Our Plans < God's Plans

Shifting Our Perspective

and Expectations

Carri Oller

God is Never Late

By Carri Oller

Copyright © Carri Oller

Cover Design: Cheryl Moore

This Book is Dedicated to...

The loves of my life Matt, Abram and Hallie. I adore
you all so much. Matt you are my knight in shining
armor. You are my absolute favorite! I'm so thankful
that God brought us together! You are the best husband
and father to our children. I love you so very much.

Abram and Hallie I'm so proud to be your mommy! I
love you both so much. I love watching God work in
your lives and watching you both grow in your
relationship with Jesus!

Contents

Chapter 1: Not What I Planned

Chapter 2: Divine Roadblocks

Chapter 3: The Right Way

Chapter 4: God's Timing

Chapter 5: Accepting God's No

Chapter 6: Carrying Out God's Yes

Chapter 7: Importance of Prayer

Chapter 8: God's Plans > My Plans

Chapter 1
Not What I Planned

At the end of 2019 I did what I always do…I made plans for the upcoming year of 2020. I had big aspirations and dreams. I even picked my "word" for 2020. For the past five years, I've asked God to give me a focus word for the year. For 2020 the word that God gave me was "vision." I can't even begin to tell you how my vision has completely shifted in 2020 already and it's only March! I made goal lists and knew exactly how I was going to achieve those goals.

Little did I or anyone else know what was about to unfold in our world causing crippling fear and chaos. The Coronavirus disease (COVID-19) was going to cause fear, panic, isolation, and anxiety throughout our Nation and throughout the world. The world watched as the virus spread like wildfire turning into a pandemic.

This was something that no one thought could really be a possibility. There's been movies made about something like this happening, but I think all of us thought that it was just that…something that only happens in movies. Yet here we all were watching our "normal" slip through our fingers like grains of sand. Each grain of sand representing our freedom.

And just like that…businesses started shutting down, restaurants shut down or went to a drive-through only protocol, schools started shutting down, churches started shutting their doors and going to church online, sporting events, The Olympics, conferences and big events such as concerts shut down. People were instructed to not be in groups bigger than ten people. People were encouraged to stay home to "break the curve" to keep the virus from spreading and to wear face masks and gloves.

This was becoming our new "normal." News updates everyday of cases of the virus spreading. It broke my heart to see people isolate and keep a distance from people. God created us in such a way that we crave being around people and community. It doesn't matter if you're an introvert or extrovert, we all crave human relationships in our lives. We all want to love and be loved. We weren't meant to be an island…we were meant for more. I would go to the grocery store and people wouldn't smile. It was as if people were sizing each other up thinking that there was bound to be someone there with the virus. All I felt was fear and anxiousness flooding each isle of the grocery store. There were a few diamonds in the rough that would smile and give a head nod of encouragement. But more often than not, fear and anxiety flooded the stores.

One day I had to go get a couple of grocery items. I didn't want to go to stores that were overcrowded. The one store that didn't have the overcrowding was my favorite store ever…Target! So I decided I would go to Target and get my items as quickly as I could and go home. My mom ended up meeting me at the store and parked her car beside mine, so she could watch my kids for me when I went in the store.

When I came back to the car my mom asked me what was wrong. I told her that it broke my heart how people interacted with each other now. No one says hello. Everyone avoids you like the plague. I honestly felt like I was in an apocalypse movie. I caught myself getting so frustrated because everything in life changed…everything was so messed up…but One remained unshaken and unchanged…God.

The Silver Lining

Some might say with all this going on it was too hard to see the silver lining. One night my sweet daughter Hallie was baking chocolate chip cookies. I encouraged her to put foil down on the cookie sheet. I did this because quite frankly I was being lazy. I didn't want to have to deal with a huge clean up. So Hallie did what I asked her to do, so little did we know the foil that we used would cause the cookies to burn on the bottom. They weren't just burned…they were charcoal. My daughter even took a picture of my husband holding one of the burnt charcoal cookies. We were all a little bummed, because we were in the mood for a sugary treat.

So I decided to speak up…I said to my husband and children, "You know sometimes we make plans and they don't work out the way we think they should. But the amazing thing about God is that He always makes things work out better than we plan. So why don't we take a family field trip to the bakery and pick out a treat?" And just like that what seemed to be a disappointment turned into a fun opportunity to do something different together.

This obstacle turned opportunity created a beautiful memory for our family. It was a teachable moment for our children to learn that sometimes things don't work out the way we think they should. There's unplanned circumstances that can happen, but it actually turns out for the better. As the days went by things started progressing. The cases of Coronavirus (COVID-19) started to rise. The death toll started to rise. Panic started to rise. We all had a choice to make…we could stay in a mindset of worry and anxiousness…or we could choose to see the silver lining.

Family Walks & Bike Rides

I think one of the biggest blessings during all the chaos was the precious quality time with my family. We were now in a position that forced us to slow down. The kids were at home with the school being closed. All activities that were planned for after school were canceled. We were in a position where we had to find things to do from home. Because let's be honest…you can only watch so much television and do things in doors.

We needed another outlet to distract us from the chaos. So we all decided to go on daily walks with our dogs. We also went on bike rides. Before all this happened, I hadn't been on a bicycle in over thirteen years. I guess you could say it was one of those things on my to do list, I was just "too busy" to make time to do it. What sweet memories we created on our walks and bike rides. The conversations, the laughter and the times of being so annoyed with each other that the sound of breathing could set us off. (Just being honest!) These are memories that I will keep with me forever.

During this time of being still there was also a lot of opportunities to think and re-evaluate what was really important in our lives. Before all of this chaos we worried about things that really didn't matter. That's when God truly shifted our perspective. I think that's also when the light bulb went off. God was using all of this to refocus our vision. Somehow along the way I think my vision got blurry. I loved God and served God, but I don't think I truly pursued God.

That's when I had a come to Jesus meeting. That's when the reality set in. I loved Jesus and served Him, but I forgot to pursue Him. I forgot the importance of pursuing Christ in my life. It broke my heart knowing that all the things I was doing for Him almost became more important than actually intentionally pursuing Him. When that realization hit me I was watching church online with my family. It was during worship and my heart completely broke. I asked God to forgive me. That wasn't ever my intention, but somehow I let my flesh get the best of me. My prayer all the time is to have a heart after God's heart, yet I wasn't really practicing what I was praying or preaching.

20/20

Anyone that knows me knows that I am a complete extrovert. I thrive and get energized by being around people. This entire situation of staying home to "break the curve" was extremely hard. At first I absolutely loathed the thought of just staying home and not having any company over. I love to entertain and one of my giftings is hospitality. So with that being said, my heart is full when my house is full. Even though this was going to be hard, it was very necessary. I needed this time to gain 20/20 vision. I needed to slow down and be still. I needed to re-evaluate what was important in my life. I needed to have clarity in my walk with Jesus. I needed to spend quality time with my husband and children. I needed to realize that instant gratification isn't always what is best for me.

Before this pandemic happened I was worried about so many things that in the end didn't really matter. I needed the scales to fall off of my eyes to realize that even though my heart loved the Lord and served Him, I wasn't truly pursuing Him. With my fast-paced life I forgot to slow down and rest in Him. I somehow allowed my vison to get out of focus. I can confidently tell you now that my vision is refocused. Each day the news pulls at our attention and fills us with fear and anxiousness. All the while, God's voice is whispering hope to us. The reason God's voice is a whisper is because He is close to us…

Are you listening?

Encouragement Scriptures

"But you must continue to believe this truth and stand firmly in it. Don't drift away from the assurance you received when you heard the Good News. The Good News has been preached all over the world, and I, Paul, have been appointed as God's servant to proclaim it."

Colossians 1:23; NLT

"I will bless the Lord who guides me; even at night my heart instructs me. I know the Lord is always with me. I will not be shaken, for he is right beside me."

Psalm 16:7-8; NLT

"I love you, Lord; you are my strength. The Lord is my rock, my fortress, and my Savior; my God is my rock, in whom I find protection. He is my shield, the power that saves me, and my place of safety."

Psalms 18:1-2; NLT

"In times of trouble, may the Lord answer your cry.
May the name of the God of Jacob keep you safe from
all harm."

Psalms 20:1; NLT

"Even when I walk through the darkest valley, I will
not be afraid, for you are close beside me. Your rod and
your staff protect and comfort me."

Psalms 23:4; NLT

Journaling My Thoughts

This section of the book is for you to journal any thoughts that you have. There's no right or wrong way to journal. However the Lord leads you is perfectly okay. I pray that you will get in a habit of journaling. I try to do this every day and it's very therapeutic for me, I think it will be for you too.

Reflection Questions

The idea for this section of the book is for you to use these questions as a time of reflection in your life. These questions are also great to use as discussion questions if you're reading this book with a friend. It's also great if you should choose to use this book as a Bible Study.
Enjoy!

1) Have you truly been pursuing Christ in your life? Can you relate to what Carri was saying?

____

____

____

____

____

2) It can be so easy to focus on what is going wrong in our lives. Carri talks about the importance of silver lining in our lives. What silver lining is in your life right now?

____

____

____

____

3) In times of trouble or uncertainty, why is it easy or hard to place our complete trust in God?

____

____

____

____

4) What things in your life have you taken for granted?
What can you do in your life to change that?

____

____

____

____

____

5) What are some areas in your life that you need to get
refocused in? What can you do to get 20/20 vision in
your life?

____

____

____

____

____

Prayer

"Dear Heavenly Father, please give me clarity and focus. So many things try to pull for my attention. Help me keep my gaze on you Jesus. Help me Lord when I am focusing on everything going wrong in my life to refocus on You. Help me drown out the noise of this world and focus on your voice. Amen."

Chapter Two

Divine Roadblocks

When I started writing this book I got stuck. I felt like I had a huge roadblock. I had prayed and prayed. God gave me the title and idea for the book. But as I started writing nothing was happening. I mean my mind was totally blank. What I didn't realize at the time is that God was getting me ready for what was about to unfold in my own life.

God was giving me an opportunity to live out what He was going to have me write about. Believe me when I say it wasn't in my plans to live out what God was going to have me write about, but it was all in God's perfect plans. So as backwards as this may sound, I actually designed my cover first completely before the interior of my book was even written. This definitely wasn't my plan, but as I said God's plans and His timing are always perfect.

Have you ever been in a hurry to get somewhere and it seemed as though you caught every single red light and roadblock? Frustrating isn't it? I will be the first one to tell you that the Jesus gets tested in me when I seem to hit every detour and red light known to man. My flesh gets the best of me. When this happens to me I'm usually running behind and my plans aren't looking like I thought they would. Let's just say that I definitely wouldn't want someone to be recording my words and actions when this happens. Sound familiar? Maybe you can relate…and maybe you're judging me…either way I'd bet to say we all have some work to do in the patience department.

I think we get this way with God too. When He doesn't do what we have prayed for. When it seems as though one thing after another is going wrong. When our present situation doesn't look like the promises that we've held dear to. Here's what I know to be true though…God's ways are so much higher than our ways. God almost NEVER does things the way we think He is going to. He ALWAYS exceeds our expectations. We can make our plans, but ultimately God's plans prevail. God has the final word.

There's been several times in my life where I felt like one delay after another would happen. It's frustrating because even though I'm a free spirit most of the time, I also am a planner. (And a control freak!) I like to know what is going to happen and when. With both of my children I scheduled to get induced, because I wanted to know what day they would be born. I also wanted to have a game plan so that we could get all of our ducks in a row before meeting our babies! I wanted the house cleaned. I wanted the dishes and laundry done. I wanted to take a shower before going to the hospital and pick out the "perfect outfit" to wear. I wanted to have my legs shaved and toenails painted. I wanted my family and friends to be there. So naturally I talked my doctors into allowing me to get induced. #ControlFreak #OhMyStars #CarriOllerBeCrayCray #FocusCarri #GetBackToThePoint #WhySoManyHashtags

So when I say that I do not like delays…I mean I DO NOT LIKE DELAYS! I don't like roadblocks and detours. However as I've matured in my faith in the Lord, I've come to understand that the delays are actually blessings in disguise. I think sometimes we think that God can't work in the dead ends. We think that if we are still that automatically means we are stuck. I'm here to tell you that's a lie from the enemy.

Selah

One day I was having a pity party for myself. I was frustrated because I felt like God had me in a season of being still. Honestly I just felt like I was stuck in a box and couldn't get out of it. I was having a get together for women in ministry at my house and expressed to each of them that for whatever reason I just felt completely stuck. I couldn't see and understand what God was doing in this season that I was in. I felt as though God forgot all about me. Which is completely untrue. God is always with us. He isn't putting us on call waiting. He isn't split with his attention towards us. I decided to get my Bible out and read. I knew that if I would get in God's Word, God would help me gain clarity. I was studying in Psalms and I happened to be on Psalm forty-six that day.

"God is our refuge and strength, a helper who is always found in times of trouble. Therefore we will not be afraid, though the earth trembles and the mountains topple into the depths of the seas, though its water roars and foams and the mountains quake with its turmoil. There is a river—its streams delight the city of God, the holy dwelling place of the Most-High. God is within her; she will not be toppled. God will help her when the morning dawns. Nations rage, kingdoms topple; the earth melts when He lifts His voice. The Lord of Armies is with us; the God of Jacob is our stronghold. Come, see the works of the Lord, who brings devastation on the earth. He makes wars cease throughout the earth. He shatters bows and cuts spears to pieces; He sets wagons ablaze. "Stop your fighting, and know that I am God, exalted among the nations, exalted on the earth. The

*Lord of Armies is with us; the God of Jacob is our
stronghold."*

Psalm 46; CSB

After reading these scriptures a few times all the way
through I started feeling God's peace come over me like
a flood. I needed that gentle reminder that God is my
refuge and strength. That wasn't the only thing that God
was showing me that day. I noticed a word beside the
scriptures that I never really paid much attention to
before. It was the word Selah. I thought to myself,
"What does that mean?" So naturally I looked it up.
Selah is an expression that is found in the Old Testament
seventy-four times. Some scholars have interpreted
Selah to be an interlude, musical pause or even a change
of voice. (Like a cry or shout) Which makes complete
sense being that this word was used in Psalms seventy-
one out of the seventy-four times.

So with Selah meaning to pause, God was gently
getting my attention. I'm here to tell you that there is a
blessing in the moments and seasons of being still. My
grandpa had the "gift of relaxation." I say it was a gift
because this world we live in is so fast paced and craves
instant gratification. Grandpa didn't mind slowing down
and being still. My grandma was the opposite. Grandma
was always doing something. Whether it was playing in
her church band or going to play cards with her friends,

grandma was always up for doing something different.
(I am A LOT like grandma in that way. I love going out
and doing fun things with family and friends!)

One day grandma wanted to go do some shopping.
So you want to know what my grandpa did? He brought
a folding chair with him and something to prop his feet
up, so that he could relax when grandma went shopping.
That's exactly what he did. He didn't care what anyone
thought about it. He just got his chair propped up and
simply relaxed. I think we could all learn a lot from my
grandpa. It's okay to be still sometimes. It's okay to be
in a season that isn't quick paced. We are always
constantly trying to rush through everything. We've got
to learn to simply pause. We've got to be still and relax
and know that God has us in the palm of His mighty
hands.

Praise in Troubled Times

As I dug more into God's Word, I looked through
Psalms to see everywhere I could find the word Selah. I
decided to start at the beginning of Psalms. I noticed
that the first time it says the word Selah was in Psalms 3.
Now to give you some background on this particular
Psalm, I'm going to give you the Carri paraphrased
version of it.

Here it goes…David is running, hiding and praying that God will save him from his enemies. One of David's biggest enemies was his own son Absalom. Absalom wanted David's throne and he was willing to kill his own father to get the throne. Absalom gathered an army of traitors that wanted to take David down. As King, David could have depended on his army to defeat his son and traitors that called themselves an army, but instead he chose to rely on God's strength in a time of crisis. David took time to pause and turn his prayers into praise.

"Lord, how my foes increase! There are many who attack me. Many say about me, "There is no help for him in God." But you, Lord, are a shield around me, my glory, and the one who lifts up my head. I cry aloud to the Lord, and he answers me from his holy mountain. I lie down and sleep; I wake again because the Lord sustains me. I will not be afraid of thousands of people who have taken their stand against me on every side. Rise up, Lord! Save me, my God! You strike all my enemies on the cheek; you break the teeth of the wicked. Salvation belongs to the Lord; may your blessing be on your people." Psalm 3:1-8; CSB

Wow, after reading those scriptures it's so encouraging to see a faith displayed like that. David knowing that his own flesh and blood wanted him dead and wanted his throne. David took time to pray and

pause. He shouted out his praises to the Lord. This isn't
the first time David turned to God in the midst of
trouble. When David was younger he also displayed this
same kind of faith when chaos of depression and anxiety
was abounding within King Saul. Before David was
king he was simply a shepherd boy who tended his
sheep. God's mighty hands and favor were on him.
David was known for his skills on the harp. When King
Saul was wrestling with a tormenting spirit within him,
he was given the advice to get someone to play songs of
worship to silence the tormenting spirit. That's where
David came in the picture.

*"Now the Spirit of the Lord had left Saul, and the
Lord sent a tormenting spirit that filled him with
depression and fear. Some of Saul's servants said to
him, "A tormenting spirit from God is troubling you. Let
us find a good musician to play the harp whenever the
tormenting spirit troubles you. He will play soothing
music, and you will soon be well again." "All right,
Saul said. "Find me someone who plays well and bring
him here." One of the servants said to Saul, "One of
Jesse's sons from Bethlehem is a talented harp player.
Not only that—he is a brave warrior, a man of war, and
has good judgement. He is also a fine-looking young
man, and the Lord is with him." So Saul sent
messengers to Jesse to say, "Send me your son David,
the shepherd." Jesse responded by sending David to*

Saul, along with a young goat, a donkey loaded with bread, and a wineskin full of wine. So David went to Saul and began serving him. Saul loved David very much, and David became his armor bearer. Then Saul sent word to Jesse asking, "Please let David remain in my service, for I am very pleased with him." And whenever the tormenting spirit from God troubled Saul, David would play the harp. Then Saul would feel better, and the tormenting spirit would go away."

1 Samuel 16:14-23; NLT

When David was younger he used worship to calm King Saul as he was being tormented. David definitely had his faults, but he also had a heart after God's. David knew the importance of that communication with God through prayer and worship. I wonder how many of us sing praises when troubles come at us from all sides. I wonder how many of us lift up our hands and say, *"God I don't know the outcome, but I know that you are God and You are good!"* I wonder how many of us lift up our hands in praise when our teenagers come at us with the wrath of what I like to call "the attitude from hell." (Don't judge me.) If you have a teen or preteen you know exactly what I'm talking about.

I don't know about you, but there have been more times than I'd like to admit that I have turned to people, things and even myself to give me comfort in tough circumstances. I sometimes forget to lift up my hands and praise the only One who deserves all praise, honor and glory. We have got to start looking at our problems in the light of God's power rather than trying to look at God in the shadows of our problems.

When we allow our problems to be magnified bigger than our God, we are misconceiving what the reality really is. The reality is there isn't any problem, obstacle or circumstance that God can't handle. Nothing is too big for Him. When everything seems like it's going wrong, God is still there for us. If God is for us than who or what can be against us? No roadblock or dead end can stop what God has for us. Even when we can't see it and it's hard to believe it. God is ultimately in complete control.

My prayer is that whatever you are facing now you will have unexplainable peace in your life. When you feel like you have no strength left. When you feel like obstacles are closing in on you like a flood, you will cry out to God in worship. Just like David cried out to God when all hell was breaking loose in his life. There's power in prayer and worship. The enemy flees when we worship and pray. There's no room for the darkness when we are choosing to consume ourselves with the light.

Remember the valley is always between two mountains. It may feel like the valley that you are in is lasting forever. I promise you that if you are in the valley, a mountain is coming. You never know how God will use the valley for the mountain that He has for you. David had to press into his faith when the valley seemed long and the promises seemed to fade into the night. All the struggles that David faced in the valley prepared him for the mountains that God had planned for him. God has good plans for you with hope and a future. Hold onto Him and don't let go. It's easier sometimes said than done. Believe me I totally get it. But I can tell you from my personal experience that it's definitely worth it.

Encouragement Scriptures

"Don't worry about anything; instead pray about everything. Tell God what you need and thank him for all he has done. Then you will experience God's peace which exceeds anything we can understand. His peace will guard your hearts and minds as you live in Christ Jesus."

Philippians 4:6-7; NLT

"I am leaving you with a gift—peace of mind and heart. And the peace I give is a gift the world cannot give. So don't be troubled or afraid."

John 14:27; NLT

"I will praise the Lord at all times. I will constantly speak his praises."

Psalms 34:1; NLT

"And now, dear brothers and sisters, one final thing.
Fix your thoughts on what is true, and honorable, and
right, and pure, and lovely, and admirable. Think about
things that are excellent and worthy of praise."

Philippians 4:8; NLT

"Rejoice in our confident hope. Be patient in trouble
and keep on praying."

Romans 12:12; NLT

Journaling My Thoughts

This section of the book is for you to journal any thoughts that you have. There's no right or wrong way to journal. However the Lord leads you is perfectly okay. I pray that you will get in a habit of journaling. I try to do this every day and it's very therapeutic for me, I think it will be for you too.

Reflection Questions

The idea for this section of the book is for you to use these questions as a time of reflection in your life. These questions are also great to use as discussion questions if you're reading this book with a friend. It's also great if you should choose to use this book as a Bible Study.
Enjoy!

1) What are some roadblocks you have had in your life that God actually used for your good?

____

____

____

____

____

2) Why is it hard for us to trust God in the middle of the storms we face? What are some truths that you hold onto when you are in the middle of a storm?

____

____

____

____

____

3) Why is it important to be still? Why is important to pray and praise when chaos and storms seem to surround us?

____

____

____

____

____

4) Is it easy or hard to praise in the middle of the storm?

____

____

____

____

____

5) What are some things we can all learn from David?

____

____

____

____

____

Prayer

"God help me in the middle of the storm. Give me strength to shout out praises even when I don't feel like it. Give me the endurance to not give up hope. Thank you Lord for always being with me. Thank you for never leaving my side. Give me clarity when sorrow tries to rob me of my peace. I love you Lord. Amen."

Chapter Three
The Right Way

All through life we have to learn lessons. Some lessons hurt worse than others. There are so many lessons I've learned in my thirty-four years of life and I know that I'll continue learning until I go home to be with the Lord. My Grandma was ninety-nine years old when she went to go home to be with the Lord. Before she passed away, she told me that she was still learning things every single day. With lessons I've learned there's usually two things…a right way to handle something and a wrong way to handle something. Unfortunately, I've had to learn many times from doing things the wrong way.

For instance when I was younger I went to a youth event at my church. At this particular youth event I had an argument with someone, and we were at odds with each other. I felt horrible about what had happened. At the end of the weekend event we were allowed to get on the microphone in front of our youth group and tell about what God had done in our lives that weekend.

This was one of those moments I learned something the hard way. (I think about it now and it just makes me cringe! I can't believe I did this! But I was an immature teenager with a big heart. I just didn't know how to handle it the right way.) I saw this opportunity as an opportunity to apologize to this person that I was at odds with. I told everyone what God had done in my life during this event and at the end of me sharing I did something…I apologized to this person publicly…IN FRONT OF EVERYONE…ON THE MICROPHONE! Needless to say that person was embarrassed, because I apologized in front of everyone and this made them even more mad at me than they were originally.

I learned in that moment that when you have a disagreement with someone, you should go to them one on one and work things out. An apology isn't meant to put someone on the spot, it's meant to reconcile, grow and heal relationships. I've also learned along the way that if you have a disagreement with someone don't try to argue, tell someone they upset you or reconcile through text messages. It's paramount that you talk face to face with someone if they have hurt you, or you have hurt them or if you are just frustrated with someone. When reading text messages you can't see the person's facial expression or hear their tone and text messages can get very misconstrued.

I've also learned that when someone has hurt you or you have hurt them it's so important to work things out as soon as possible. The more time that you allow pass by before working things out with someone, the more you allow the enemy to plant bitterness and take root in your life. *"And don't sin by letting anger control you." Don't let the sun go down while you are still angry, for anger gives a foothold to the devil." Ephesians 4:26-27; NLT*

Unfortunately sometimes no matter what you do some people won't forgive or try to reconcile. Some people through their own brokenness will gaslight you or make you feel like you should own every part of the argument, instead of owning their part in it. They are always the victim and you are the "bad guy" every single time. I've learned that with these particular kinds of people you have to say you're sorry for your part, forgive them for their part and move on even if that means you don't get complete closure about the situation at hand…even if that means that you don't get an *"I'm sorry too."*

Even if that means people gossip untruths about you and your integrity. Even if that means that they hold a grudge against you. There's freedom in forgiveness. There's freedom in letting go. There's complete freedom in giving those relationships and situations to

God. He's more than strong enough to handle anything that comes our way.

In Our Flesh

There are millions and I mean millions (I'm not exaggerating…I'm a hot mess express) of other examples of lessons I could tell you that I've learned and I'm still learning. One thing remains true, there's a right and wrong way to handle situations and people. When we choose to handle things our own fleshly way instead of pressing into God and seeking His guidance in our lives, we will stumble over and over again. We also stumble by doing things our own way and ignore the wisdom that we gain through God's Word in our lives.

I can't even begin to tell you how many times I've tried to figure out situations or relationships in my own strength without seeking God. Guess what? Every single time I do this it doesn't work. It never works. It always falls apart and always ends up breaking my heart in the process. This also happens when I put all of my trust and faith in imperfect people rather than placing all of my faith and trust in the perfect and one true God.

I've also learned the importance of having people that are more seasoned in their walk with Christ in my life and people that are older in my life that can speak truth over me. If you don't have those people in your life, I encourage you to get those people in your life. Join a Bible Study or small group at church. You will never understand the value of having someone like this in your life until you've experienced it yourself. When you have someone that has had more life experience than you, they can pour their life experiences into you and you can learn from their triumphs and mistakes.

Can't All Go with You

Sometimes in school a teacher will allow you to retake a test that you make a low score on. In school that was the best thing ever. (I was given this opportunity in school more than a time or two. #JustKeepinItReal) It was like you got a second chance to make things right and to make things better. God is so faithful in doing this too. However, it's not always fun. From experience I can tell you that it's never fun to retake "the test."

When God called me to do this ministry of writing and speaking I was scared. I didn't feel qualified or good enough. I doubted every step I took. I was completely terrified. You see I never liked to be alone when I was younger. My mom and dad would always laugh, because when I was younger I always had a friend

with me everywhere I went. My mom even said that
when she told me I couldn't go hang out with friends
until my bedroom was cleaned. It wouldn't be more than
ten minutes later, and a friend would ring our doorbell
and ask if they could help me clean my bedroom. I
thrived and got energy when I was around others. I
guess you could say it was like a safety blanket for me to
be around others. To be honest, I feel like at times I was
co-dependent on others.

One day as I was on this journey of pursuing God
and His plans for me, I found myself getting frustrated. I
was frustrated because I had this come to Jesus moment
that I didn't necessarily want to realize. I was starting to
do what I did when I was younger. I was talking to my
husband about being frustrated and feeling hurt. I was
frustrated and hurt because every time I thought God
brought me someone to help me in ministry, something
would always block it or fall apart.

I started crying and weeping out of frustration and
bewilderment. That's when the Holy Spirit spoke loud
and clear to me through my sweet husband. After
patiently listening to my griping and complaining about
the situations at hand, my husband looked at me with
such love. He took a deep breath and said, *"Carri don't
you see the pattern here? It's quite obvious. The reason
that you feel like things fall apart or get blocked is
because you keep trying to bring the people God didn't*

intend for you to bring with you. God didn't call these people to do what He's called you to do. When God gave you the dream He put in your heart, didn't He give it to YOU? If He did then why do you keep trying to take people with you? Babe sometimes you just can't take everyone with you to where God is calling you."

This divine conversation and godly wisdom that my sweet husband was having with me stopped me in my tracks. It was as if in that moment God was having a heart to heart with me. I felt like the light bulb came on in that moment and the blinders came off. I realized that I was falling into some of the unhealthy patterns of leaning too much on people rather than completely leaning on God. It's so important to have people that love and care about you in your life that will call you out when you need to be called out. It's also equally important to be teachable and open to hear godly wisdom and advice. I'm thankful that my husband was listening to the Holy Spirit in his response to me that day. Lord knows I needed it! #JustKeepinItReal

We Do Need Each Other

Now please hear me…I'm not saying that we shouldn't lean on each other. I'm not saying that we don't need people to help us along the way. I'm saying that if we are leaning more on people than we are leaning on God then we are out of order. Unfortunately even with my good intentions of serving the Lord, I was doing that exact thing. I was putting more of my trust in people than God. I've also learned that God will bring the right people to help and serve beside you.

It is important to have people in your life to lean on. Even Jesus had the twelve disciples to help Him in His ministry. I thank God for my inner circle of people that I can pray with and we encourage one another. In fact I have a thing I do at my house once a month called "Coffee Chat." This is a time where I just invite a lot of my friends to come and hang out. Everyone brings a snack to share and I have the coffee bar and coffee creamers. Several of us go to different churches and are in different walks of life, but this is a time where we can all just come together, talk about the Lord and pray for one another. I also encourage my friends to bring someone with them that normally doesn't go to church. It's a neutral ground that isn't overwhelming to a non-church goer or a non-believer. It's a sweet time of laughter, encouragement and fellowship.

If you don't have something like this in your life, can I encourage you to get plugged in? Get plugged into a small group or Bible Study at church. Or start something like "Coffee Chat" at your house. Or start a group that meets at your favorite coffee shop or restaurant. Surround yourself with like-minded people that are pursuing Jesus in their lives. In this broken world we live in, we need accountability and encouragement.

Encouragement Scriptures

"Your word is a lamp to guide my feet and a light for my path."

Psalms 119:105; NLT

"Then Jesus said to his disciples, "If any of you wants to be my follower, you must give up your own way, take up your cross and follow me."

Matthew 16:24; NLT

"But don't just listen to God's word. You must do what it says. Otherwise, you are only fooling yourselves."

James 1:22; NLT

"Understand this, my dear brothers and sisters: You must all be quick to listen, slow to speak, and slow to get angry."

James 1:19; NLT

"Listen to my instruction and be wise. Don't ignore it."

Proverbs 8:33; NLT

"Commit yourself to instruction; listen carefully to words of knowledge."

Proverbs 23:12; NLT

Journaling My Thoughts

This section of the book is for you to journal any thoughts that you have. There's no right or wrong way to journal. However the Lord leads you is perfectly okay. I pray that you will get in a habit of journaling. I try to do this every day and it's very therapeutic for me, I think it will be for you too.

Reflection Questions

The idea for this section of the book is for you to use these questions as a time of reflection in your life. These questions are also great to use as discussion questions if you're reading this book with a friend. It's also great if you should choose to use this book as a Bible Study.
Enjoy!

1) How can you relate to what Carri was saying about leaning more on people rather than leaning completely on God?

____
____
____
____
____

2) What are some "tests" that you've had to retake in your life? How has God helped you pass the "test?"

____

____

____

____

____

3) Who are some people in your life that have helped you and encouraged you? Who have you helped and encouraged lately? What can you do to encourage others?

____

____

____

____

____

4) Have you ever had an argument using text messages?
How did that work out for you? Why is it important to
reconcile with someone face to face rather than through
text messages?

____

____

____

____

____

5) What are some ways that God is trying to get your
attention right now by going the right way instead of the
wrong way?

____

____

____

____

____

Prayer

"Dear Lord, forgive me Lord when I choose the wrong way. Forgive me Lord when I put you on the backburner. Thank you for putting all my broken pieces back together again. Thank you for giving me grace even when I don't deserve it. Lord put people in my life that will speak truth to me and encourage me. Help me be an encouragement to others. Speak to me Lord and guide my steps. Amen."

Chapter Four
God's Timing

I can't even begin to tell you how many times I've preached, taught, written and talked about how God's timing is perfect. If I'm being totally honest, I'd have to confess that there have been equally (if not more) as many times that I doubted, gave into fear and got frustrated with God. I was frustrated because God wasn't working on my timetable. He also wasn't doing the things that I wanted or planned. I'm so thankful for God's grace and patience with me. #hotmessexpresspartyofone

Sound familiar? Maybe you can totally relate to what I'm saying and maybe you can't. But I'd bet to say that more people than not can 100% relate to what I'm saying. During this time of being in quarantine something happened…I got my eyes on the setbacks and allowed the confusion of the unknown future get me down. I allowed myself to give into some of my old ways where I tried to figure every little thing out. #RecoveringControlFreak #ConstantWorkInProgress

I tried to tell God what I thought was supposed to happen and when. Oh man. That stung a little…okay a lot while typing that. I also had another conversation with God about how I didn't understand how things were going to work. I got in my own way. I then started making a "Plan B" because I felt like God wasn't making "Plan A" happen. #humblingmomentforCarri

If I were God and I had to deal with my flaws and questioning, I would seriously lose my ever-loving mind. I mean I would seriously want to karate chop me directly in the jugular…SERIOUSLY DIRECTLY IN THE JUGULAR. But God is such a good and patient Father. He sees us battle with our flesh. He sees us with all of our faults, yet He still died on the cross for us. He tells us He wants us. He is with us and wants to use us to spread His truth. Yet here I am knowing deep in my heart what is true yet, giving into the lies of the evil one. I let my flesh get the best of me. The uncertainties around me were never bigger than the certainty of God around me, beside me, in front of me, or behind me.

Shut Up and Listen

God always gives a word when we are at the end of our rope. We just have to be willing to shut up a minute and listen. Yes I said it. God gave us one mouth and two ears. Why? Because listening is so very important. It's not only important to listen to God, but to each other too. I finally chose to stop having a pity party where captain pity and captain complainer were the party planners. I chose to pray and ask God to guide me.

I remember as I was praying and battling the doubts and fears and I was trying to come up with a backup plan incase God didn't come through on the original plan…Yikes! That was even harder to admit and type. How can I doubt God when He has constantly shown Himself faithful time and time again? Let's be honest…God is God and I'm just well…me! God has always been and will always be. I was born in 1986 and someday I will breathe my last breath on earth. This body will get tired and wear out. God however will never wear out. He is the Alpha and the Omega, the beginning and the end. So how can I honestly doubt God's plans and abilities? Even though I was in this battle of control and complete surrender, God saw that I was in desperate need of clarity and confirmation. I got a message from my friend's sister. She said, *"Life is a bit crazy right now. I always turn to your books when I get stressed or overwhelmed. No matter what I'm going through that day, I'll just grab one of your books and start reading. All of them bring me so much comfort. It's helped me to learn to trust and give it all to God. Please never stop writing!"*

Now, I'm sure you can imagine how I felt when I received that message. I felt like in that exact moment God reminded me why I was doing what I was doing. That message was exactly what I needed to keep going. I went from searching for a different avenue to take "plan b" and remembering what God put on my heart "plan a." It's amazing what happens when we pray and ask God for clarity, direction and simply be still and listen. In fact many times God will give us multiple confirmations. Especially when we can tend to be a little stubborn like myself. #justkeepinitreal

Another sweet friend of mine texted me and said, *"I read some of your book and it felt like I was listening to a close friend from across a table for coffee or lunch. So sweet and love reading your book, it's very intimate and personal. Thank you! I'm going to send you a video that I felt God led me to share with you. It relates to your writing and other giftings that you feel it may speak into."* The amazing thing about both of these confirmations is that these two people don't know each other, yet they both confirmed similar things and said what I needed to hear to keep moving forward.

Here's the thing…I think God speaks to us and confirms things all the time to us. Unfortunately we can miss the mark by overanalyzing, overthinking and trying to figure everything out on our own. We allow ourselves to get in our own way and block the blessing that God is trying to give us. Maybe you've been struggling with that lately. Maybe you've been trying to figure everything out on your own. Maybe you're feeling worn and empty. Can I tell you something? It's time to wave that white flag and surrender to God's perfect will for your life. It's time to lean on God and trust that His plans for your life are bigger and better. God's plans most of the time don't look anything like we plan, but God takes everything and uses it for our good. All of the hardships and obstacles shape us, refine us and prepare us for what God has for us.

Get Away From Me

I say this all the time, but the disciple Peter is seriously my favorite disciple. He's my favorite because I can relate to him in so many ways. He had a pure heart and loved the Lord, but sometimes his questioning and doubting got in the way of the breakthrough God was trying to give him. *"From then on Jesus began to tell his disciples plainly that it was necessary for him to go to Jerusalem, and that he would suffer many terrible things at the hands of the elders, the leading priests, and the teacher of religious law. He would be killed but on the third day he would be raised from the dead. But Peter took him aside and began to reprimand him for*

*saying such things. "Heaven forbid Lord," he said.
"This will never happen to you!" Jesus turned to Peter
and said "Get away from me, Satan! You are a
dangerous trap to me. You are seeing things merely
from a human point of view, not from God's." Matthew
16:21-23; NLT.* You see in this moment Peter forsook
God's plans and perspective and evaluated the situation
from a human perspective. Jesus rebuked Peter because
Peter's attitude and perspective were coming from a
place of fear and doubt…not faith.

What is super crazy about this incident with
Peter, was that he literally just confessed and said that
Jesus was the Messiah. *"When Jesus came to the region
of Caesarea Philippi, he asked his disciples, "Who do
people say that the Son of Man is?" "Well," they.
Replied, "some say John the Baptist, some say Elijah,
and others say Jeremiah or one of the other prophets."
Then he asked them, "But who do you say I am?" Simon
Peter answered, "You are the Messiah, the Son of the
living God." Jesus replied, "You are blessed, Simon son
of John, because my Father in heaven has revealed this
to you. You did not learn this from any human being.
Now I say to you that you are Peter (which means rock),
and upon this rock I will build my church, and all the
powers of hell will not conquer it. And I will give you
the keys of the Kingdom of Heaven. Whatever you forbid
on earth will be forbidden in heaven, and whatever you*

permit on earth will be permitted in heaven." Then he sternly warned the disciples not to tell anyone that he was the Messiah." Matthew 16:13-20; NLT

It was almost as if Peter was speaking out of both sides of his mouth. On one hand Peter said that Jesus was the Messiah, the Son of God. On the other hand he spoke fear and doubt over Jesus' suffering and death. What's even more interesting is that Jesus knew what Peter was about to do, yet he called Peter a "rock" where He was going to build his church. Jesus revealed Peter's identity and role even though he knew what Peter was about to do. That my friend is what you call grace. Sweet amazing undeserved grace.

I'm so thankful for grace. I'm thankful for the grace that God gives me on a daily basis. I'm thankful for the grace my husband and children give me when I fall short…which happens a lot. You know what else is a blessing? Giving grace to someone else and giving grace to ourselves. When you give someone grace, you are being an example of what God does for you daily. When you give yourself grace, you set yourself free from the chains of condemnation that have been holding you down for far too long.

What grace are you in need of today?

Who do you need to give grace to today?

Encouragement Scriptures

"Be still and know that I am God! I will be honored by every nation. I will be honored throughout the world."

Psalms 46:10; NLT

"But don't just listen to God's word. You must do what it says. Otherwise, you are only fooling yourselves."

James 1:22; NLT

"Understand this, my dear brothers and sisters: You must all be quick to listen, slow to speak, and slow to get angry."

James 1:19; NLT

"Commit yourself to instruction; listen carefully to words of knowledge."

Proverbs 23:12; NLT

"My sheep listen to my voice; I know them, and they follow me."

John 10:27; NLT

"The Lord directs the steps of the godly. He delights in every detail of their lives. Though they stumble, they will never fall, for the Lord holds them by the hand."

Psalms 37:23-24; NLT

Journaling My Thoughts

This section of the book is for you to journal any thoughts that you have. There's no right or wrong way to journal. However the Lord leads you is perfectly okay. I pray that you will get in a habit of journaling. I try to do this every day and it's very therapeutic for me, I think it will be for you too.

Reflection Questions

The idea for this section of the book is for you to use these questions as a time of reflection in your life. These questions are also great to use as discussion questions if you're reading this book with a friend. It's also great if you should choose to use this book as a Bible Study.
Enjoy!

1) Carri said that sometimes she lets her flesh get the best of her when it comes to trusting God. Are you letting your flesh get the best of you? What are the things or situations that you need to trust God in your life?

____

____

____

____

____

2) Have you ever tried to come up with a backup plan incase God didn't come through with what He told you? How did that work out for you? What did you learn through that experience?

____

____

____

____

____

3) Have you ever been desperate for clarity or direction in your life? How did God come through when you were facing those situations in your life?

____

____

____

____

____

4) What are some things in your life that you need to let
go of and surrender to God? Is it easy or hard for you to
give those things to God?

____

____

____

____

____

5) Who do you need to give grace to right now in your
life? Do you need to give yourself grace?

____

____

____

____

____

Prayer

"Dear Lord, help me listen to your voice above all the noise in this world. Forgive me Lord when I doubt the plans you have for me. Help me Lord when I feel confused and worn. Give me strength to keep going and to not give up. Help me give grace to those that have hurt me. Help me give grace to myself. Lord let your perfect will be done in my life. Amen."

Chapter Five
Accepting God's No

I think the majority of us would probably say we don't like to be told no, especially if we want something. I mean when I try to order one of my favorite beverages at Starbucks and they are out of it. (Iced matcha with extra matcha and vanilla…so good! #getbacktothepoint) I get a little frustrated, especially when I made up my mind and I knew what I wanted. I mean honestly it sounds a bit selfish and silly to get frustrated at such a tiny thing.

So what happens when God tells us no? Well if I'm going to be completely honest, when God has said, *"no"* on different things in my life I got mad. I didn't understand why God would tell me no. There would be times that later on God revealed to me why the answer was *"no,"* and quite frankly I was thankful that God told me *"no"* on those things. Then there would be times that God told me *"no"* and I didn't understand. I still to this day don't understand. It gets frustrating sometimes. Even though I get frustrated, deep in my heart I know that God has a reason for His *"no's."* We have to remember that God sees the bigger picture. We also need to remember that God is God and we are definitely not.

Embrace the Waves

I love going on vacation somewhere that is close to the beach and the ocean. My favorite thing is to walk on the beach to pick up seashells. I love the feeling of the sand between my toes and the ocean water splashing against my feet. It gives such a clear perspective that this world is so big, and we are so small. To think that the God of the universe is so much bigger than the ocean and anything in this world is amazing. The ocean is one of those things however, that I have a healthy fear of. I think that comes from the fact that my brother Robert had me watch the movie, *"Jaws"* with him and from that point forward the ocean freaks me out. Like seriously…my mom had to stay in the bathroom when I would take baths for a while because I was afraid that *"Jaws"* was going to get me in the bathtub.

When the waves of this life crash on us from all sides and we feel like we are being crushed, we have to remember that diamonds are made by being crushed. In fact the more it's crushed, the purer it is. The storms in this life aren't meant to destroy us, they are meant to help refine us. Instead of looking at our problems as problems, we should see them as opportunities for growth. It's easier said than done, believe me I know.

"Dear brothers and sisters, when troubles come your way, consider it an opportunity for great joy. For you know that when your faith is tested, your endurance has a chance to grow. So let it grow for when your endurance is fully developed, you will be perfect and complete, needing nothing. If you need wisdom, ask our generous God, and he will give it to you. He will not rebuke you for asking. But when you ask him, be sure that your faith is in God alone. Do not waver, for a person with divided loyalty is as unsettled as a wave of the sea that is blown and tossed by the wind. Such people should not expect to receive anything from the Lord. Their loyalty is divided between God and the world, and they are unstable in everything they do. Believers who are poor have something to boast about, for God has honored them. And those who are rich should boast that God has humbled them. They will fade away like a little flower in the field. The hot sun rises and the grass withers; the little flower droops and falls, and its beauty fades away. In the same way, the rich will fade away with all of their achievements. God blesses those who patiently endure testing and temptation. Afterward they will receive the crown of life that God

has promised to those who love him. And remember, when you are being tempted, do not say, "God is tempting me." God is never tempted to do wrong, and he never tempts anyone else. Temptation comes from our own desires, which entice us and drag us away. These desires give birth to sinful actions. And when sin is allowed to grow, it gives birth to death. So don't be misled, my dear brothers and sisters. Whatever is good and perfect comes down to us from God our Father, who created all the lights in the heavens. He never changes or casts a shifting shadow. He chose to give birth to us by giving us his true word. And we, out of all creation, became his prized possession." James 1:2-21; NLT

I don't know about you…but if someone came up to me and told me to rejoice when all hell was breaking loose in my life I would probably want to karate chop them in the jugular. But this is exactly what James does. He tells us to rejoice because when the waves hit us from all sides, it gives us the opportunity to grow in our walk with God. It sifts the impurities out of us. It deepens our faith and perseverance. We don't really know the depth of our character, until we are given the opportunity to test our character. That's what the *"nos"* from God give us.

As I'm writing this book, there are a lot of storms going on in my life. It's as if the waves are getting bigger and bigger. I'm planting my feet on firm foundation (Jesus) and I see the waves coming toward me. Truth be told right now in this very moment I'm feeling so heavy hearted about several things. I've been praying and asking God to lighten the load off of my shoulders. Instead of the load getting lighter, I feel like the load is getting heavier and heavier every day. Imagine standing on a rock and watching wave after wave come toward you. That's how I feel.

Is it frustrating? Yes it really is. Sometimes the load of the waves coming at me take all of my energy from me. I just want to go to my room, pull the blanket over my head and cry. (To be honest I did do that one day. #justkeepinitreal) Even though I feel like the waves are trying to wipe me out, consume and drown me, there's a hope deep within me that is unshakable. *"And the Holy Spirit helps us in our weakness. For example, we don't know what God wants us to pray for. But the Holy Spirit prays for us with groanings that cannot be expressed in words. And the Father who knows all hearts knows what the Spirit is saying, for the Spirit pleads for us believers in harmony with God's own will. And we know that God causes everything to work together for the good of those who love God and are called according to his purpose for them." Romans 8:26-28; MSG*

When we don't have the words to speak and all we can do is cry, the Holy Spirit intercedes on our behalf. Everything that I'm going through, everything that you're going through can and will be used for our good. We may not understand it. We may get a *"no"* from God. But please know this, God is for you! If God is for you and God is for me, nothing can stand against us! God always wins! Things may not turn out the way we planned or the way we wanted, but to be honest…the plans we make are nothing in comparison to the plans God has for us. We've just got to put our faith in God. When we choose to cling to worry and fear closer than we cling to God, we are telling God that we don't believe He is big enough to handle whatever situation we are going through. We've got to submit ourselves to the Lord and not our circumstances. We've got to remember that God has the final word. Believe me when I say, I'm preaching to myself here. #GuiltyAsCharged #Conviction. #MicDrop. #HelpMeJesus #HotMessExpress

Encouragement Scriptures

"Keep on asking, and you will receive what you ask for. Keep on seeking, and you will find. Keep on knocking, and the door will be opened to you. For everyone who asks, receives. Everyone who seeks, finds. And to everyone who knocks, the door will be opened."

Matthew 7:7-8; NLT

"When you go through deep waters, I will be with you. When you go through rivers of difficulty, you will not drown. When you walk through the fire of oppression, you will not be burned up; the flames will not consume you."

Isaiah 43:2; NLT

"The Lord is close to the brokenhearted; he rescues those whose spirits are crushed."

Psalm 34:18; NLT

"So be strong and courageous! Do not be afraid and do not panic before them. For the Lord your God will personally go ahead of you. He will neither fail you nor abandon you."

Deuteronomy 31:6; NLT

"You know what I long for Lord; you hear my every sigh."

Psalm 38:9; NLT

"God is our refuge and strength, always ready to help in times of trouble."

Psalms 46:1; NLT

"You are my strength; I wait for you to rescue me, for you, O God, are my fortress. In his unfailing love, my God will stand with me. He will let me look down in triumph on all my enemies."

Psalms 59:9-10; NLT

Journaling My Thoughts

This section of the book is for you to journal any thoughts that you have. There's no right or wrong way to journal. However the Lord leads you is perfectly okay. I pray that you will get in a habit of journaling. I try to do this every day and it's very therapeutic for me, I think it will be for you too.

Reflection Questions

The idea for this section of the book is for you to use these questions as a time of reflection in your life. These questions are also great to use as discussion questions if you're reading this book with a friend. It's also great if you should choose to use this book as a Bible Study.
Enjoy!

1) What are some situations or circumstances in your life that you are thankful that God told you, *"no"* in?

____

____

____

____

____

2) When reading the scriptures in James, what things
and situations came to your mind that you need to trust
God more in?

____

____

____

____

____

3) What does it mean to submit ourselves to God and
not our circumstances?

____

____

____

____

____

4) What does Deuteronomy 31:6 mean to you?

____

____

____

____

____

5) What are some things in your life that you need to fully submit to God in? When you fully submit and let go of those things to God what will you gain?

____

____

____

____

____

Prayer

"Dear Lord, the storms and waves in my life want to bring me down and make me fill empty. God remind my heart that you hear every word, you see every tear and struggle. Help me Lord when I want to try to control the things that are out of my control. Help me God focus my attention on your truth. With every wave that hits me God, help me press more into you. Amen."

Chapter Six
Carrying Out God's Yes

One day we were at my brother & sister-in-law's house celebrating my daughter & niece's birthdays. Our family get togethers are always filled with laughter, deep conversations, goofiness and craziness. This particular get together was sweeter than most. It was when we were finally all able to be together due to having to all be in quarantine with coronavirus restrictions. Just being able to finally all be together was the sweetest feeling. It brought so much joy to my heart.

Everyone was playing volleyball and my mom and dad were observing and cheering us all on. My son said he was tired of playing volleyball and wanted to swim. So I told him I'd go with him to just be sure he was safe. As my son was splashing around in the water, I found myself a comfy seat out of the sun and then something caught my eye. It was a momma bird feeding her babies. I watched as she diligently flew from her nest to find food. She flew from the nest to feed her babies to hunt for food eight times. She didn't give up.

She gave it all the energy she had. She was faithful.
Honestly it was exhausting just watching her go and
come back each time. I admired her perseverance.

That was when God got my attention. I watched
as this momma bird gave it her all. She might have been
exhausted, but she didn't quit. She had a mission to feed
her babies and that was her focus and priority. You see,
during this time of quarantine, I allowed myself to get a
little down. I then started giving into some of my old
ways of doubting and questioning God. I started trying
to come up with back up plans incase God didn't come
through, or in case I missed the mark somehow. I felt in
that moment that God quietly spoke to my heart and
said, *"If I can equip this bird to fulfill my purpose, don't
you think I can do the same with you Carri? It doesn't
matter what happens in this world. I have the final
word. Stop looking at the problems and uncertainties,
look to me for clarity and peace."* Well that stung a
little…okay it stung a lot! We have to believe in God's
faithful character. God is who He says He is, and He
does what He says He will do.

The Faithful Ones

One of my favorite books of the Bible is the book
of Hebrews. I love it because it talks a lot about faith

and keeping the faith. It talks about the importance of responding to the things that God speaks to us. We have to hold onto His promises in our lives. We demonstrate true faith when we trust in the promises of God even if they haven't materialized yet…even if we don't live to see them fully materialize. *"So do not throw away this confident trust in the Lord. Remember the great reward it brings you! Patient endurance is what you need now, so that you will continue to do God's will. Then you will receive all that he has promised. For in just a little while, the Coming One will come and not delay. And my righteous ones will live by faith. But I will take no pleasure in anyone who turns away. But we are not like those who turn away from God to their own destruction. We are the faithful ones, whose souls will be saved."* *Hebrews 10:35-39; NLT*

When reading and studying those scriptures it truly convicts my heart, as I'm sure it convicts yours as well. The question we all have to ask ourselves is are we truly being the "faithful ones?" Are we trusting and saying, "yes" to God? Or are we attempting to put God in a box when we say, "yes" to Him? I know I've been guilty of that more than a time or two. We can't put limits on a limitless God. If we truly want to see radical change in our lives and partake in the blessings God has for us, we've got to say, "yes" with a willing heart. We've got to totally surrender. We've got to be the faithful ones who will trust God in the midst of uncertainty, because God is certainty.

Faith Heroes

The Bible is filled with faith heroes that I aspire to be like. I want a radical faith that will inspire others and help others persevere. I want that kind of faith that makes the devil flee, because he knows he won't break me. I want that faith that makes the devil nervous when I get up out of bed in the morning.

I want a faith like this…

"Faith is the confidence that what we hope for will actually happen; it gives us assurance about things we cannot see. Through their faith, the people in days of old earned a good reputation. By faith we understand that the entire universe was formed at God's command, that what we now see did not come from anything that can be seen. It was by faith that Abel brought a more acceptable offering to God than Cain did. Abel's offering gave evidence that he was a righteous man, and God showed his approval of his gifts. Although Abel is long dead, he still speaks to us by his example of faith. It was by faith that Enoch was taken up to heaven without dying—"he disappeared, because God took him." For

before he was taken up, he was known as a person who pleased God. And it is impossible to please God without faith. Anyone who wants to come to him must believe that God exists and that he rewards those who sincerely seek him. It was by faith that Noah built a large boat to save his family from the flood. He obeyed God, who warned him about things that had never happened before. By his faith Noah condemned the rest of the world, and he received the righteousness that comes by faith. It was by faith that Abraham obeyed when God called him to leave home and go to another land that God would give him as his inheritance. He went without knowing where he was going. And even when he reached the land God promised him, he lived there by faith—for he was like a foreigner, living in tents. And so did Isaac and Jacob, who inherited the same promise. Abraham was confidently looking forward to a city with eternal foundations, a city designed and built by God. It was by faith that even Sarah was able to have a child, though she was barren and was too old. She believed that God would keep his promise. And so a whole nation came from this one man who was as good as dead—a nation with so many people that, like the stars in the sky and the sand on the seashore, there is no way to count them. All these people died still believing what God had promised them. They did not receive what was promised, but they saw it all from a distance and welcomed it. They agreed that they were foreigners and nomads here on earth. Obviously people who say such things are looking forward to a country they can call their own. If they had longed for the country they came from, they could have gone back. But they were looking for a better place, a heavenly homeland. That is why God is not ashamed to be called their God, for he has prepared a city for them. It was by faith that Abraham offered Isaac as a sacrifice when God was testing him. Abraham, who had received God's promises, was ready to sacrifice his only son, Isaac, even though God had told him, "Isaac is the son through whom your descendants will be counted." Abraham reasoned that if Isaac died, God was able to bring him back to life again. And in a sense, Abraham did receive his son back from the dead. It was by faith that Isaac promised blessings for the future to his sons, Jacob and Esau. It was by faith that Jacob, when he was old and dying, blessed each of Joseph's sons and bowed in worship as he leaned on his staff. It was by faith that Joseph, when he was about to die, said confidently that the people of Israel would leave Egypt. He even commanded them to take his bones with them when they left. It was by faith that Moses' parents hid him for three months when he was born. They saw that God had given them an unusual child, and they were not afraid to disobey the king's command. It was by faith that Moses, when he grew up, refused to be called the son of Pharaoh's daughter. He chose to share the oppression of God's people instead of enjoying the fleeting pleasures of sin. He thought it was better to suffer for the sake of Christ than to own the treasures of Egypt, for he was looking ahead to his great reward. It was by faith that Moses left the land of Egypt, not fearing the king's anger. He kept right on going because he kept his eyes on the one who is invisible. It was by faith that Moses commanded the people of Israel to keep the Passover and to sprinkle blood on the doorposts so that the angel of death would not kill their firstborn sons. It was by faith that the people of Israel went right through the Red Sea as though they were on dry ground. But when the Egyptians tried to follow, they were all drowned. It was by faith that the people of Israel marched around Jericho for seven days, and the walls came crashing down. It was by faith that Rahab the prostitute was not destroyed with the people in her city who refused to obey God. For she had given a friendly welcome to the spies. How much more do I need to say? It would take too long to recount the stories of the faith of Gideon, Barak, Samson, Jephthah, David, Samuel, and all the prophets. By faith these people overthrew kingdoms, ruled with justice, and received what God had promised them. They shut the mouths of lions, quenched the flames of fire, and escaped death by the edge of the sword. Their weakness was turned to strength. They became strong in battle and put whole armies to flight. Women received their loved ones back again from death. But others were tortured, refusing to turn from God in order to be set free. They placed their hope in a better life after the resurrection. Some were jeered at, and their backs were cut open with whips. Others were chained in prisons. Some died by stoning, some were sawed in half, and others were killed with the sword. Some went about wearing skins of sheep and goats, destitute and oppressed and mistreated. They were too good for this world, wandering over deserts and mountains, hiding in caves and holes in the ground. All these people earned a good reputation because of their faith, yet none of them received all that God had promised. For God had something better in mind for us, so that they would not reach perfection without us." Hebrews 11; NLT

Just Say Yes

I think what these scriptures teach us is that saying, *"Yes"* to God plays a huge role in our faith. If we can say, *"Yes"* can change not only our lives but those around us. It has a ripple effect of blessings. However, that doesn't mean that everything is going to be easy. Just because we love the Lord and say, *"Yes"* to Him doesn't mean that the path before us will be filled with "fluff" and good things all the time. On the contrary, saying *"Yes"* to God may mean that we will endure persecution, loss, pain, struggle, and to some that may even mean death.

The pain in this life is nothing compared to the blessings and joy that are coming. We've just got to keep our eyes on Jesus. When doubt and fear try to creep in and chain us to depression and anxiety, we've got to rebuke those lies from the enemy and hold onto, believe and confess the promises of God.

Listed below are some of the promises from God that are found in scripture. I pray that you will take time and look up these amazing promises in God's Word. I pray that you won't only look them up, but that you'll highlight them, memorize them and meditate on them.

Isaiah 40:29-31

Jeremiah 29:11

James 4:7

Exodus 14:14

Deuteronomy 31:8

John 3:16

James 1:5

1 John 1:9

Encouragement Scriptures

"But don't just listen to God's Word. You must do
what it says. Otherwise, you are only fooling
yourselves."

James 1:22; NLT

"Study this Book of Instruction continually.
Meditate on it day and night so you will be sure to obey
everything written in it. Only then will you prosper and
succeed in all you do."

Joshua 1:8; NLT

"If you love me, obey my commandments."

John 14:15; NLT

"When you obey my commandments, you remain in my love, just as I obey my Father's commandments and remain in his love."

John 15:10; NLT

"Joyful are those who obey his laws and search for him with all their hearts."

Psalms 119:2; NLT

"We can make our plans, but the Lord determines our steps."

Proverbs 16:9; NLT

"This foolish plan of God is wiser than the wisest of human plans, and God's weakness is stronger than the greatest of human strength."

1 Corinthians 1:25; NLT

Journaling My Thoughts

This section of the book is for you to journal any thoughts that you have. There's no right or wrong way to journal. However the Lord leads you is perfectly okay. I pray that you will get in a habit of journaling. I try to do this every day and it's very therapeutic for me, I think it will be for you too.

Reflection Questions

The idea for this section of the book is for you to use these questions as a time of reflection in your life. These questions are also great to use as discussion questions if you're reading this book with a friend. It's also great if you should choose to use this book as a Bible Study.
Enjoy!

1) What are some situations or circumstances in your life that you are thankful that you said, *"Yes"* to God in?

____

____

____

____

____

2) What are some things in your life that God is waiting for you to say, *"Yes"* in?

____

____

____

____

____

3) Why is it easier to say *"no"* to God than *"yes?"*

____

____

____

____

____

4) When reading Hebrews 11; how does it help inspire you to keep moving forward with saying, *"Yes"* to God?

____

____

____

____

____

5) Carri says, *"we've got to be the faithful ones who will trust God in the midst of uncertainty, because God is certainty."* What does it mean to be one of the faithful ones?

____

____

____

____

____

Prayer

"Dear Lord, sometimes the uncertainties of this life try to steal my focus. God help me hold onto your promises. Help me when I feel like saying, *"yes"* will be too hard and impossible. God you make impossibilities possible. You are powerful. You are mighty. You give me strength to overcome any obstacle that comes my way. I want to do what you want me to do. I want to go where you want me to go. You alone God are my clarity and my peace. Amen."

Chapter Seven
Importance of Prayer

Prayer is so important. It's important because it is how we communicate and talk with God. It's also important because whether we realize it or not, prayer also changes us. It changes our posture, our atmosphere and the situations going on around and within us. I love studying about prayer in God's Word. There's so many different kinds of prayers in The Bible that radically changed people and outcomes. I know personally that there have been times that I have prayed, and I received quick answers from the Lord. Then there's been other times where I prayed and the prayers I prayed, felt as though they were just hitting the ceiling and getting unanswered. I felt like God didn't hear me or see me in my hurt and confusion.

As I've matured in my faith, I've come to realize that God always answers. Sometimes the answer is yes. Sometimes the answer is no. Sometimes the answer is wait. We love it when God says, *"yes"* to our prayer requests. We love it because God gave us what we prayed for. Others get inspired by our answered prayer and are in awe of God's faithfulness. It becomes a testimony of what prayer can do. We dislike it when God says, *"no"* to our prayer requests. We dislike it because God didn't give us what we prayed for. We get frustrated and uncomfortable when He tells us no. We question and doubt His goodness and sovereignty, because we didn't get what we wanted or what we think we needed.

When I think about the times God has answered, *"no"* at the time He told me, *"no"* it hurt. To be honest, it was extremely frustrating. Believe me when I say, I informed God what I thought about it. I mean who am I to tell God that He didn't do what He should have done? #ConfessionsOfAHotMessExpressWoman #ThankfulGodLovesMe #ThankfulForGrace #ThisPastorNeedsJesus #GetBackToThePointCarriOller Even to this day there are things God has told me, *"no"* and I still don't understand. Here's what I do understand…those times that God answered, *"no"* pushed me even closer to Him. I prayed more, I pressed into Him more, I was filling page after page in my prayer journal, I found myself in worship more…As backwards and bizarre as it may sound, I'm thankful for the "no's" in my life…it has pushed me closer to my Heavenly Father. #BitterSweet

We also get frustrated when the answer is,
"wait." As I've confessed a million times, waiting isn't
something I like to do. If I'm being perfectly honest…I
absolutely hate it. The reason I hate it is because the
answer I'm seeking isn't happening in my timing. But
much like hearing the answer, *"no"* from God, *"wait"* is
equally important in our faith walk. When we hear,
"wait" from the Lord, it causes us to be on our knees
more in prayer. We press into God more. We long to
hear an answer from God. I've learned that when God
tells us to wait, we aren't ready for the *"yes"* or *"no"*
He's about to give us.

Perspective Shift

Many times before we get the *"yes"* or *"no"*
we've got to shift our perspective to God's perspective.
I feel like God uses the *"wait"* to prepare us for the
"yes" or *"no."* What we've all got to remember is that
it doesn't matter what situations and obstacles are
surrounding us, God surrounds it all. There's nothing
too big or too small for Him to care about and handle.
We've got to get our eyes off of the problems and
setbacks and onto the problem solver. We've got to shift
our perspective to let God direct our thoughts and

emotions, rather than giving all the power of our peace of mind to the circumstances we are facing.

We've got to remember that God would be unjust in giving us something we weren't ready or prepared for. He would also be unjust in not giving us something we are prepared and ready for. The bottom line is God has an amazing track record. He is constantly faithful. He is constantly good. He is always just. He is fair. God knows what you need more than you do. God knows you better than you know yourself. He made you. He knows every single cell in your body, every bone, every muscle, every fear, every worry…HE KNOWS YOU. He knows what you need. He has good plans for you. Prayer opens our eyes to a fresh perspective…God's perspective.

"What shall we say about such wonderful things as these? If God is for us, who can ever be against us? Since he did not spare even his own Son but gave him up for us all, won't he also give us everything else? Who dares accuse us whom God has chosen for his own? No one—for God himself has given us right standing with himself. Who then will condemn us? No one—for Christ Jesus died for us and was raised to life for us, and he is sitting in the place of honor at God's right hand, pleading for us. Can anything ever separate us from Christ's love? Does it mean he no longer loves us if we have trouble or calamity, or are persecuted, or hungry,

*or destitute, or in danger, or threatened with death? No,
despite all these things, overwhelming victory is ours
through Christ, who loved us. And I am convinced that
nothing can ever separate us from God's love. Neither
death nor life, neither angels nor demons, neither our
fears for today nor our worries about tomorrow—not
even the powers of hell can separate us from God's love.
No power in the sky above or in the earth below—
indeed, nothing in all creation will ever be able to
separate us from the love of God that is reveled in Christ
Jesus our Lord." Romans 8:31-39; NLT*

Prayer Life

Our pastor and dear friend Bryan said this
amazing one liner one day while teaching about prayer at
church. He said, *"The level of your perspective is
directly attached to the level of your prayers."* When I
heard that it was as if the Lord had a megaphone right
next to my ear. I had to reevaluate my prayer life in that
moment. I had to figure out where my prayer life was.
Was I going through the motions? Or was I praying
authentic and raw prayers? Was I praying prayers of
faith knowing that God could do the "impossible?" Or
was I praying and worrying about the outcome, rather
than trusting that God had it all in His mighty hands?
Maybe right now you are doing the same thing after

reading that. So I have to ask… how's your prayer life?
What does your prayer life look like? Do you only pray
when you need something? Is prayer part of your daily
life? Do you see the true value and importance of prayer
in your life? I know these are some "in your face"
questions, but they are important questions that you and I
need to ask ourselves daily.

Prayer of Jabez

There's a man named Jabez in the Bible. What's
interesting about Jabez is that he isn't well known for
some heroic duty in the Bible. He isn't well known for a
huge mistake in the Bible. He is well known by his
prayer to the Lord. *"And Jabez called on the God of
Israel saying, "Oh, that You would bless me indeed, and
enlarge my territory, that Your hand would be with me,
and that You would keep me from evil, that I may not
cause pain!" So God granted him what he requested."
1 Chronicles 4:10; NKJV*

What I love about Jabez is that this simple prayer
that he prayed changed his perspective (the name he was
given and what was spoken over him) and the outcome
of his life. You see, the word Jabez in Hebrew actually
means; distress or pain. Even though Jabez walked
around with his name meaning something that sounds a

bit like a curse or a dark cloud that should have followed him everywhere, he was actually known to be more honorable then his brothers that are listed in the Bible.

We can all learn a lot from this simple prayer of Jabez. Jabez asked God to bless him. He asked God to help him and be with him in his work by expanding his territory. And finally he asked God to keep him from causing trouble and pain. It wasn't some drawn out prayer that sounded all religious or performance based. It was a simple prayer from the heart. That's all God really wants. He wants us to come to Him with our concerns, our worries, our fears, our praises, and anything and everything we have on our mind. He loves and cares about us. How amazing is it that we get to talk to God whenever we want? Even more so, how amazing is it that the God that designed the universe knows our name and cares about us?

Quick Yes

Have you ever prayed about something and God answered you with, *"yes"* quickly? There have been several times in my life that God answered, *"yes"* so quick that when I got my answer, it almost knocked me off my feet. There have been people in my life that prayed for something and when they actually got what

they prayed for; they almost didn't know what to do with
the *"yes"* they were given. It was as if they prayed for it
not thinking that God would actually give them what
they prayed for.

*"About that time King Herod Agrippa began to
persecute some believers in the church. He had the
apostle James killed with a sword. When Herod saw
how much this pleased the Jewish people, he also
arrested Peter. Then he imprisoned him, placing him
under the guard of four squads of four soldiers each.
Herod intended to bring Peter out for public trial after
the Passover. But while Peter was in prison, the church
prayed very earnestly for him. The night before Peter
was to be placed on trial, he was asleep, fastened with
two chains between two soldiers. Others stood guard at
the prison gate. Suddenly, there was a bright light in the
cell, and an angel of the Lord stood before Peter. The
angel struck him on the side to awaken him and said,
"Quick! Get up!" And the chains fell off his wrists.
Then the angel told him, "Get dressed and put on your
sandals." And he did. "Now put on your coat and
follow me," the angel ordered. So Peter left the cell,
following the angel. But all the time he thought it was a
vision. He didn't realize it was actually happening.
They passed the first and second guard posts and came
to the iron gate leading to the city, and this opened for
them all by itself. So they passed through and started*

walking down the street, and then the angel suddenly left him. Peter finally came to his senses. "It's really true!" he said. "The Lord has sent his angel and saved me from Herod and from what the Jewish leaders had planned to do to me!" When he realized this, he went to the home of Mary, the mother of John Mark, where many were gathered for prayer. He knocked at the door in the gate, and a servant girl named Rhoda came to open it. When she recognized Peter's voice, she was so overjoyed that, instead of opening the door, she ran back inside and told everyone, "Peter is standing at the door!" You're out of your mind!" they said. When she insisted they decided, "It must be his angel." Meanwhile, Peter continued knocking. When they finally opened the door and saw him, they were amazed. He motioned for them to quiet down and told them how the Lord had led him out of prison. "Tell James and the other brothers what happened," he said. And then he went to another place." Acts 12:1-17; NLT

I love these scriptures in the book of Acts for several reasons. First, if you know me, read any of my books, or heard me preach before, you know that Peter is my favorite disciple. (It's because I can relate to him in a lot of ways.). I love that Peter was in such shock that he thought he was actually having a vision from the Lord being set free from prison. When in reality God was actually freeing him from prison. (This is so something I would do. I would be like…wait…what? Is this for real?) I also love how when Peter went to Mary's house that when Rhoda went to answer the door and heard Peter's voice, she could hardly believe it. She even left Peter standing outside! They were all in amazement that God answered their prayers for Peter to be set free from King Herod. Here's what we've all got to remember; God always answers our prayers…sometimes the answer is *"yes,"* sometimes the answer is *"no,"* and sometimes the answer is simply *"wait."*

Encouragement Scriptures

"Confess your sins to each other and pray for each other so that you may be healed. The earnest prayer of a righteous person has great power and produces wonderful results."

James 5:16; NLT

"But when you pray, go away by yourself, shut the door behind you, and pray to your Father in private. Then your Father, who sees everything, will reward you."

Matthew 6:6; NLT

"Never stop praying."

1 Thessalonians 5:17; NLT

"And the Holy Spirit helps us in our weakness. For example, we don't know what God wants us to pray for. But the Holy Spirit prays for us with groanings that cannot be expressed in words."

Romans 8:26; NLT

"I also tell you this: If two of you agree here on earth concerning anything you ask, my Father in heaven will do it for you."

Matthew 18:19; NLT

"The Lord has heard my plea; the Lord will answer my prayer."

Psalms 6:9; NLT

"Praise God, who did not ignore my prayer or withdraw his unfailing love from me."

Psalms 66:20; NLT

Journaling My Thoughts

This section of the book is for you to journal any thoughts that you have. There's no right or wrong way to journal. However the Lord leads you is perfectly okay. I pray that you will get in a habit of journaling. I try to do this every day and it's very therapeutic for me, I think it will be for you too.

Reflection Questions

The idea for this section of the book is for you to use these questions as a time of reflection in your life. These questions are also great to use as discussion questions if you're reading this book with a friend. It's also great if you should choose to use this book as a Bible Study. Enjoy!

1) Why is prayer important in your daily life? Are you praying daily?

____

____

____

____

____

2) What does it mean to shift our perspective to God's perspective?

____

____

____

____

____

3) Carri says, *"What we've all got to remember is that it doesn't matter what situations and obstacles are surrounding us, God surrounds it all."* What does that mean to you knowing that God surrounds it all?

____

____

____

____

____

4) What did you learn from reading the Prayer of Jabez?

____

____

____

____

5) *"The level of your perspective is directly attached to the level of your prayers."* What does this quote mean to you?

____

____

____

____

____

Prayer

"Dear Lord, thank you for always listening to my prayers. Thank you for never giving up on me, even when I gave up on you out of fear, doubt and worry. I want my prayer life and my faith in You to be strong Lord. Give me strength. Give me wisdom. Just like Jabez prayed Lord, expand my territory. Protect me Lord. Guide me. Keep me from all evil and harm Lord. God I trust you. Amen."

Chapter Eight

God's Plans > My Plans

God's plans are always bigger than my plans. God sees the bigger picture. We are so limited in what we can see, yet for whatever reason we still doubt God's abilities and trust more in our own abilities. God has been faithful a long time. He will continue to be faithful. He invites us to simply have faith in Him. He doesn't call us to be perfect, we simply have to be willing and trust Him. *"Trust in the Lord with all your heart; do not depend on your own understanding. Seek his will in all you do, and he will show you which path to take."* *Proverbs 3:5-6; NLT*

If I make a list of all the things that have happened in my life that weren't in my plans, the list would be extremely long. Even though the majority of those things weren't in my plans and most of them were painful to go through, those times of hurt and confusion are the very things that brought me closer to Jesus. Not only did my faith grow in those times, but the depth of my relationship with Jesus grew through it all. I wouldn't change a thing. I'm thankful for the refining fires of this world that we get to go through.

Set Free

Before Jesus died on the cross, He had a big heart to heart with His disciples. When I say they had a "come to Jesus meeting," they really did! Jesus warned the disciples that they would be facing persecution because of their faith in Him. He also told them that He was about to die on the cross and why He was doing that. (So that we can be set free from sin forever!) This was also the time where Jesus introduced the Holy Spirit to His disciples.

"I have told you these things so that you won't abandon your faith. For you will be expelled from the synagogues, and the time is coming when those who kill you will think they are doing a holy service for God. This is because they have never known the Father or me. Yes, I'm telling you these things now, so that when they happen, you will remember my warning. I didn't tell you earlier because I was going to be with you for a while longer. But now I am going away to the one who sent me, and not one of you is asking where I am going. Instead, you grieve because of what I've told you. But in fact, it is best for you that I go away, because if I don't,

*the Advocate won't come. If I do go away, then I will
send Him to you. And when He comes, He will convict
the world of its sin, and of God's righteousness, and of
the coming judgement. The world's sin is that it refuses
to believe in me. Righteousness is available because I
go to the Father, and you will see me no more.
Judgement will come because of the ruler of this world
has already been judged. There is so much more I want
to tell you, but you can't bear it now. When the Spirit of
truth comes, He will guide you into all truth. He will not
speak on His own but will tell you what He receives from
me. All that belongs to the Father is mine; this is why I
said, "The Spirit will tell you whatever He receives from
me." John 16:1-15; NLT*

What I love about these scriptures is that Jesus is
telling His disciples that even though they wanted Him
there with them, He had a much bigger plan then what
they could see. He also gave them a warning about what
was to come through the persecution they would endure
because of their faith in Him. Jesus also assured them
that no matter what they would face, or where they
would go, the Holy Spirit was going to be there to help
them and guide them.

If the disciples had their way, they would have
kept Jesus there with them. They didn't want to lose
Him. However, God had bigger plans than they could
see or comprehend. Jesus had to die so that we could be

saved. Even though the disciples didn't feel like watching Jesus die on the cross was something that they wanted to witness, they learned that it was necessary so that we can all be set free. *"For God loved the world so much that he gave his one and only Son, so that everyone who believes in him will not perish but have eternal life. God sent his Son into the world not to judge the world, but to save the world through him." John 3:16-17; NLT*

What I love about these scriptures is the simplicity and truth behind them. All we have to do is believe in Jesus to be saved. We don't have to check off a list of things that we can't ever measure up to. We simply have to believe and trust in Him. There is no other religion around that has grace given like that. That is the beauty of Christ.

What Would You Do?

Before I started writing books and speaking full time, I was a youth pastor in Oklahoma City. I got asked this question a few times from my students, and to this day that question stays with me. The question was, *"If you could go back in time and change the bad things that have happened to you, would you change them?"* That question stopped me in my tracks. I really had to think about it…would I change them? The conclusion I came up with was, *"No I wouldn't change a thing."* That may seem weird. That may seem bizarre, but it's the truth.

I wouldn't change anything in my life; the good, the bad, or the ugly. I would keep it all. Now, you may be reading this and think to yourself, *"Why wouldn't you change the bad things? Why would you want to go through all that you have been through?"* I think that my answer is simply this; I'm glad I went through what I've gone through, because it shows others that what I have gone through didn't break me…it made me stronger. It made me better. It drew me closer to Jesus. Each season of life I've gone through, has prepared me for the next season of life I'm going to go through. God is faithful that way. He prepares us whether we realize it or not.

What would you do? Would you want to change those tough seasons that you are going through or that you've been through in your life? Before you quickly answer, *"Yes please!"* I want you to think about something…if you changed the tough seasons that you've experienced in your life, would you be as strong as you are now? Would you be as empathetic towards others that have gone through or are going through similar things? Would you be seeking Jesus as deeply? I can't answer for you, but I can answer for myself…My answer to those questions would be, *"No I wouldn't."*

All of the real-life events in The Bible that are recorded are full of ups, downs, and everything in between. I guarantee that if we were to ask those whose lives we learn from each time we open God's Word, if they would want to change the things they went through, they would answer, *"No I wouldn't change a thing."* The reason I think they would give that answer is because of the millions and billions of people that their testimonies have blessed. Sometimes the things we go through aren't just a growth opportunity and lesson for us, but it's also a growth opportunity and lesson for others.

Change is Necessary

If I'm being totally honest, I don't really like change if I'm not in control of the things that are changing. I like the feeling of something being familiar. When changes happen in my life, it's almost as if I'm a snow globe and someone shakes me, and everything seems chaotic around me. Change gets me out of my groove. Even though I'm not the hugest fan of change, I know that it's necessary for my growth.

God doesn't want us to be stagnant. He wants us to grow in our walk with Him. He wants us to be the best version of ourselves that we can be. He wants us to

walk through each season of our lives prepared and
ready for whatever comes next. For that to fully happen
in our lives change is necessary. When you walk
through changes in this life, remember that God is with
you. He won't leave you or forsake you.

God's Plans

In this very moment as I'm typing this book,
there are several different things pulling my attention
and focus. There are doors that my family and I have
been praying to open, and they seem to be shut right
now. We just received some news that wasn't what we
were hoping to hear. There are people that I love that are
going through several severe health issues right now.
My kids are home with me 24-7 which I love, but when
they start arguing and going crazy…this momma waves
her white flag and says, *"I need a break!"* This season
that my family and I are in right now is a tough season,
but we know that God has the final word over it all.

*"My thoughts are nothing like your thoughts," says the
Lord. "And my ways are far beyond anything you could
imagine. For just as the heavens are higher than the
earth, so my ways are higher than your ways and my
thoughts higher than your thoughts. The rain and snow
come down from the heavens and stay on the ground to*

*water the earth. They cause the grain to grow,
producing seed for the farmer and bread for the hungry.
It is the same with my word. I send it out, and it always
produces fruit. It will accomplish all I want it to, and it
will prosper everywhere I send it. You will live in joy
and peace. The mountains and hills burst into song, and
the trees of the field will clap their hands! Where once
there were thorns, cypress trees will grow. Where
nettles grew, myrtles will sprout up. These events will
bring great honor to the Lord's name; they will be an
everlasting sign of his power and love."*

Isaiah 55:8-13; NLT

A Walking Billboard

We all have choices to make. We all can choose
to let events and situations in our lives make us bitter or
better. We all are walking billboards. We all have a
choice to be a person that fills and builds people up or
sucks the life out of the people around us. What kind of
walking billboard are you? Here's what kind of walking
billboard I have been at times. I've been the person that
wallows in self-pity and bitterness. I've been the person
that walked around with a huge chip on my shoulder.
I've been the person that got hurt by some of my
brothers and sisters in Christ, so I put up walls around

me so I wouldn't get hurt. I've been the person that was running on fumes and had nothing else in me to give. I've been the person who was angry, confused and broken. I've also been the person that blamed God for my circumstances. That's not the type of billboard I want people to see when they look at my life.

By God's grace and His alone, I've also been the person that others leaned on in times of crisis. I've been the person that boldly talked about what Jesus has done in my life. I've been the person that stood up for what is right. I've been the person that trusted God in uncharted waters. I've been the person who prayed and prayed for those around me to get saved. I've been the person that gave encouragement to those around me. I've been the person that praised God in the midst of the storms I was facing. I've been the person that trusted God and stepped out of the boat in faith. That's the kind of person that I pray people see. I want to be that kind of billboard for the Lord.

The bottom line is this…we all have a choice to make. We all get to choose what kind of billboard for the Lord we are going to be. We all fall short, but that's not the part that matters. What matters is if you get back up and seek God with all the strength you have in you. We all are given a certain amount of time on this earth. What are you doing with your time? What are you doing with your energy? What are you doing with your resources? What are you doing with your talents? What words are you confessing with your mouth? What kind of billboard are you going to be? Are you going to trust in God's plans?

Maybe someone gifted you this book, maybe you saw this book and thought it might be interesting, maybe you are borrowing this book, whatever the case may be…I want you to know I prayed for you. I pray that every person that reads this book is blessed. I pray that this book can help someone on their faith journey. *"For everyone who calls on the name of the Lord will be saved." Romans 10:13; NLT*

If you've never prayed to receive Jesus as your personal
Lord and Savior before, I want to invite you to do that
right now.

Dear Lord,

*Thank you for loving me. Lord forgive me for my sins.
Thank you for dying on the cross for my sins Jesus. I
want to live my life with you as my Savior. Thank you
for loving me and never giving up on me. Amen.*

If you prayed this prayer I want to be one of the
first ones to say, *"Welcome to the family!"* The Bible
says that when one person repents and asks Jesus to be
their Lord and Savior, the angels celebrate. *"Or suppose
a woman has ten silver coins and loses one. Won't she
light a lamp and sweep the entire house and search
carefully until she finds it? And when she finds it, she
will call in her friends and neighbors and say, "Rejoice
with me because I have found my lost coin." In the same
way, there is joy in the presence of God's angels when
even one sinner repents." Luke 15:8-10; NLT*

Encouragement Scriptures

"Be thankful in all circumstances, for this is God's will for you who belong to Christ Jesus."

1 Thessalonians 5:18; NLT

"May he equip you with all you need for doing his will. May he produce in your, through the power of Jesus Christ, every good thing that is pleasing to him. All glory to him forever and ever! Amen."

Hebrews 13:21; NLT

"For our present troubles are small and won't last very long. Yet they produce for us a glory that vastly outweighs them and will stand forever! So we don't look at the troubles we can see now; rather, we fix our gaze on things that cannot be seen. For the things we see now will soon be gone, but the things we cannot see will last forever."

2 Corinthians 4:17-18; NLT

"So humble yourselves before God. Resist the devil, and he will flee from you."

James 4:7; NLT

"Then if my people who are called by my name will humble themselves and pray and seek my face and turn from their wicked ways, I will hear from heaven and will forgive their sins and restore their land."

1 Chronicles 7:14; NLT

"Show me the right path, O Lord; point out the road for me to follow. Lead me by your truth and teach me, for you are the God who saves me."

Psalm 25:4-5; NLT

"The Lord is good, a strong refuge when trouble comes. He is close to those who trust in him."

Nahum 1:7; NLT

Journaling My Thoughts

This section of the book is for you to journal any thoughts that you have. There's no right or wrong way to journal. However the Lord leads you is perfectly okay. I pray that you will get in a habit of journaling. I try to do this every day and it's very therapeutic for me, I think it will be for you too.

Reflection Questions

The idea for this section of the book is for you to use these questions as a time of reflection in your life. These questions are also great to use as discussion questions if you're reading this book with a friend. It's also great if you should choose to use this book as a Bible Study.
Enjoy!

1) What things in your life has God used to bring you closer to Him?

____

____

____

____

____

2) Carri says, *"I'm thankful for the refining fires of this world that we get to go through."* Are you thankful for the refining fires? Why or why not?

____

____

____

____

____

3) What does Isaiah 55:8-13 mean to you?

____

____

____

____

____

4) What kind of walking billboard are you? What kind
of walking billboard do you aspire to be?

____

____

____

____

____

5) What are you doing with your time? What are you
doing with your talents? What are you doing with your
resources?

____

____

____

____

____

Prayer

"Dear Lord, thank you for loving me. Thank you Lord for dying for me, so that I can be set free. Lord help me be a walking billboard that points to you in all that I think, say, and do. Lord I want to please you with my life. I want to honor you in all that I do. Help me God be bold and courageous for your namesake. Thank you God for being with me always. Thank you for refining me through everything that I've been through. I love you Lord. Amen."

More Books by Carri Oller:

God Uses the Unusable

Foundation Strong

Enjoy the Journey

Letting Go of What I Can't Control

Silenced in Jesus Name

Unfamiliar Heroes: Autism "The Unkept Secret"

God is Never Late

Website: www.carrioller.com